DANGEROUS MAMMALS

AFRICAN BUFFALO

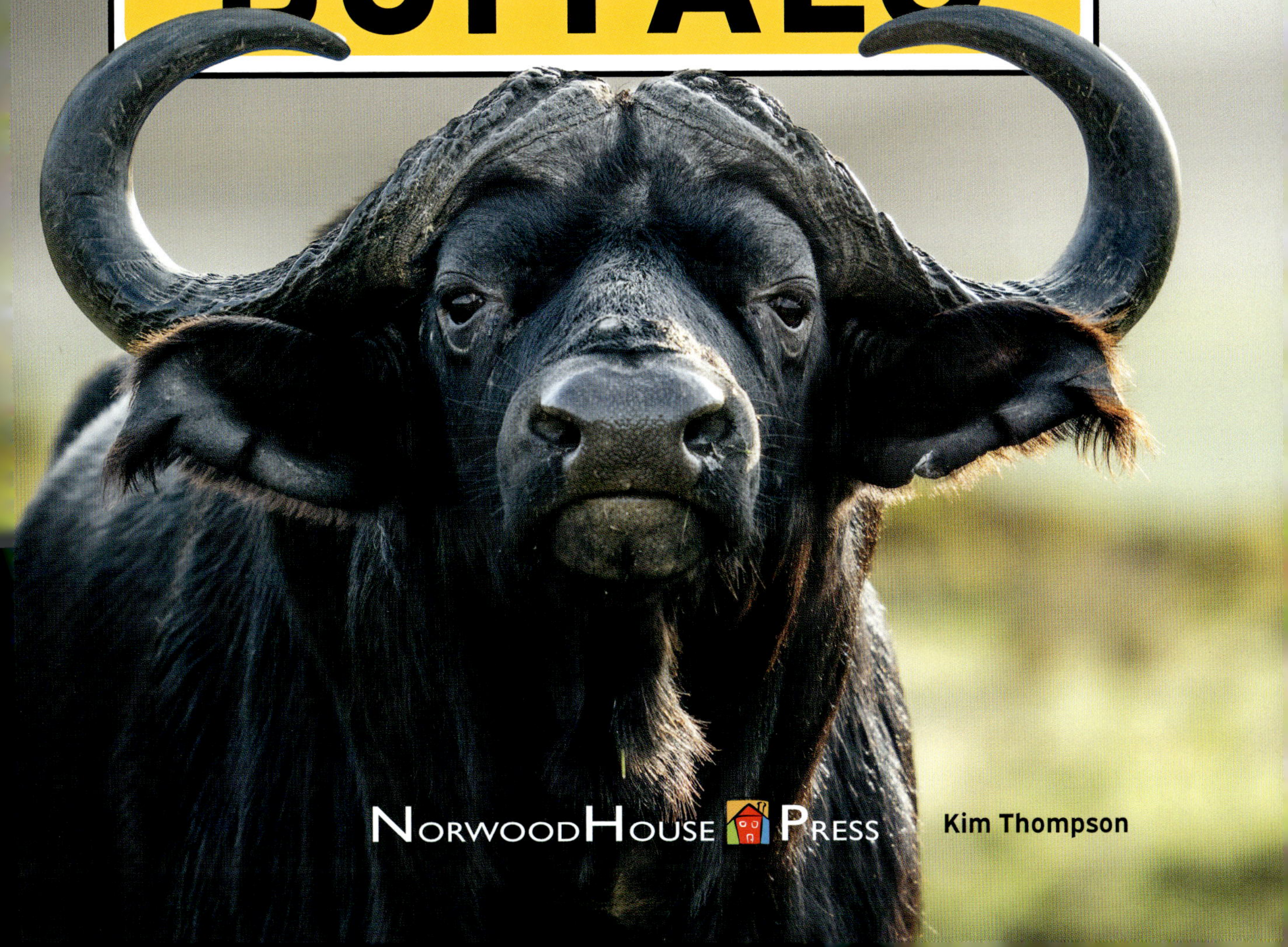

NorwoodHouse Press

Kim Thompson

Cataloging-in-Publication Data

Names: Thompson, Kim, 1970-.
Title: African buffalo / Kim Thompson.
Description: Buffalo, NY : Norwood House Press, 2026. | Series: Dangerous mammals | Includes glossary and index.
Identifiers: ISBN 9781978577527 (pbk.) | ISBN 9781978577534 (library bound) | ISBN 9781978577541 (ebook)
Subjects: LCSH: African buffalo--Juvenile literature.
Classification: LCC QL737.U53 T474 2026 | DDC 599.642--dc23

Published in 2026 by
Norwood House Press
2544 Clinton Street
Buffalo, NY 14224

Designer: Rhea Magaro

Photo credits: Cover, p. 1 E.T Roets/Shutterstock.com; p. 5 Martin Prochazkacz/Shutterstock.com; p. 6 kyslynskahal/Shutterstock.com; p. 7 Seyms Brugger/Shutterstock.com; p. 8 lemaret pierrick/Shutterstock.com; p. 9 Vaclav Sebek/Shutterstock.com; p. 10 Michal Hamet/Shutterstock.com; p. 11 matthieu Gallet/Shutterstock.com; p. 12 AnnaBaranova/Shutterstock.com; p. 15 Thomas Torget/Shutterstock.com; p. 16 PACO COMO/Shutterstock.com; p. 17 Four Oaks/Shutterstock.com; p. 18 Rudi Hulshof/Shutterstock.com; p. 19 LouieLea/Shutterstock.com; p. 21 Marc_H/Shutterstock.com

Printed in the United States of America

CPSIA compliance information: Batch #CWNHP26: For further information contact Norwood House Press at 1-800-237-9932.

TABLE OF CONTENTS

MEET THE AFRICAN BUFFALO

African buffalo are large **mammals**. Their feet have **hooves**. Big horns grow from their heads.

They can be nearly six feet (two meters) tall and 11 feet (three meters) long. They can weigh 2,000 pounds (900 kilograms).

Buffalo live in **herds**. Most herds have a few hundred animals. Some have thousands!

Herds help protect buffalo from attacks by lions and other predators.

TYPES OF AFRICAN BUFFALO

There is just one **species** of buffalo in Africa. It is divided into four **subspecies**.

Southern Savanna Buffalo

The southern savanna buffalo is the largest and most well-known. It is also called the Cape buffalo.

West African savanna buffalo and central African savanna buffalo are closely related to Cape buffalo. They all live on **savannas**.

Savanna buffalo have hook-shaped horns. At their base, the horns can grow together. This forms a shield over the animal's forehead that is called a boss.

Forest Buffalo

The forest buffalo is the smallest African buffalo. It lives in rainforests and other wet areas. This buffalo has reddish-brown fur. Its short horns curve straight up.

FAVORITE FOOD

African buffalo are **herbivores**. They eat grass. They spend most of their time grazing.

Birds such as oxpeckers sometimes get a ride. They help buffalo by eating insects from their hair.

STAYING SAFE AROUND AFRICAN BUFFALO

Buffalo are huge. They are also fast. They can run 37 miles (60 kilometers) per hour.

These animals get upset easily. It is hard to know how they will react. For all these reasons, buffalo are very dangerous! Some people call Cape buffalo "black death."

When buffalo get upset, they **charge**. They use their horns as weapons.

African buffalo **gore** and kill hundreds of people every year.

Buffalo herds need lots of space. Towns and buildings get in their way and put people in danger.

Never go toward buffalo. Keep a safe distance away from these giant animals.

GLOSSARY

charge (chahrj): to attack in a rush

gore (gor): to stab or wound with something sharp, such as a horn

herbivores (HUR-buh-vorz): animals that eat only plants

herds (hurdz): groups of animals that live and travel together

hooves (huvz): the hard parts on the feet of some animals like horses, cows, and buffalo

mammals (MAM-uhlz): animals that are warm-blooded, have hair or fur, and feed milk to their babies

savannas (suh-VAN-uhz): grasslands with few or no trees that are found in warm places on Earth

species (SPEE-sheez): a group of animals that are alike and that can have babies together

subspecies (SUHB-spee-sheez): smaller groups within a species that are slightly different from each other

THINKING QUESTIONS

1. Why do buffalo live in herds?
2. What is the habitat of the Cape buffalo?
3. What do African buffalo eat?
4. Why are African buffalo dangerous?
5. How can you stay safe around buffalo?

INDEX

ABOUT THE AUTHOR

Kim Thompson has been an animal lover ever since she was little. She loves to watch animals and photograph them, especially in the wild. She thinks that learning about animals can inspire people to take actions that help animals survive on the planet we share.